Roneka Taylor

OUR MOMMY HAD CANCER

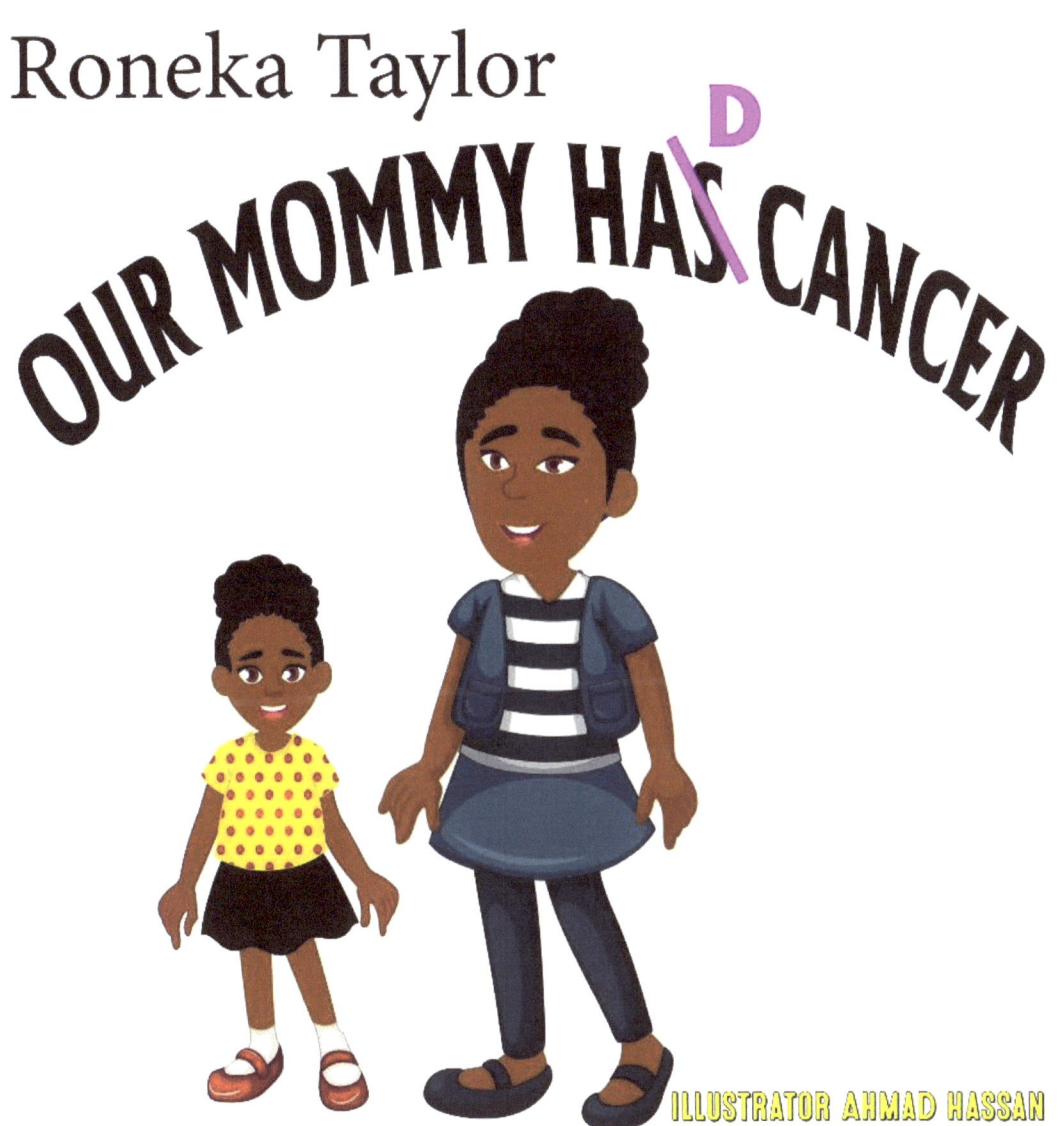

ILLUSTRATOR AHMAD HASSAN

Copyright © 2021 by Roneka Taylor
All rights reserved.
No part of this book may be used or reproduced
in any manner whatsoever without the prior
permission of the author.
Published in the United States
by Strength Builders Publishing LLC
strengthbuilderspublishing.com
ISBN 978-1-7368052-9-9

Dedication

I wrote this book for my babies Cortney, Coryn, Ryco, and EVERYONE who prayed for me during my journey. It is because of you all that I am here today as a Breast Cancer SURVIVOR! My prayer is that my journey will encourage someone behind me to keep going.

Mommy felt two small lumps in her breasts while in the shower.

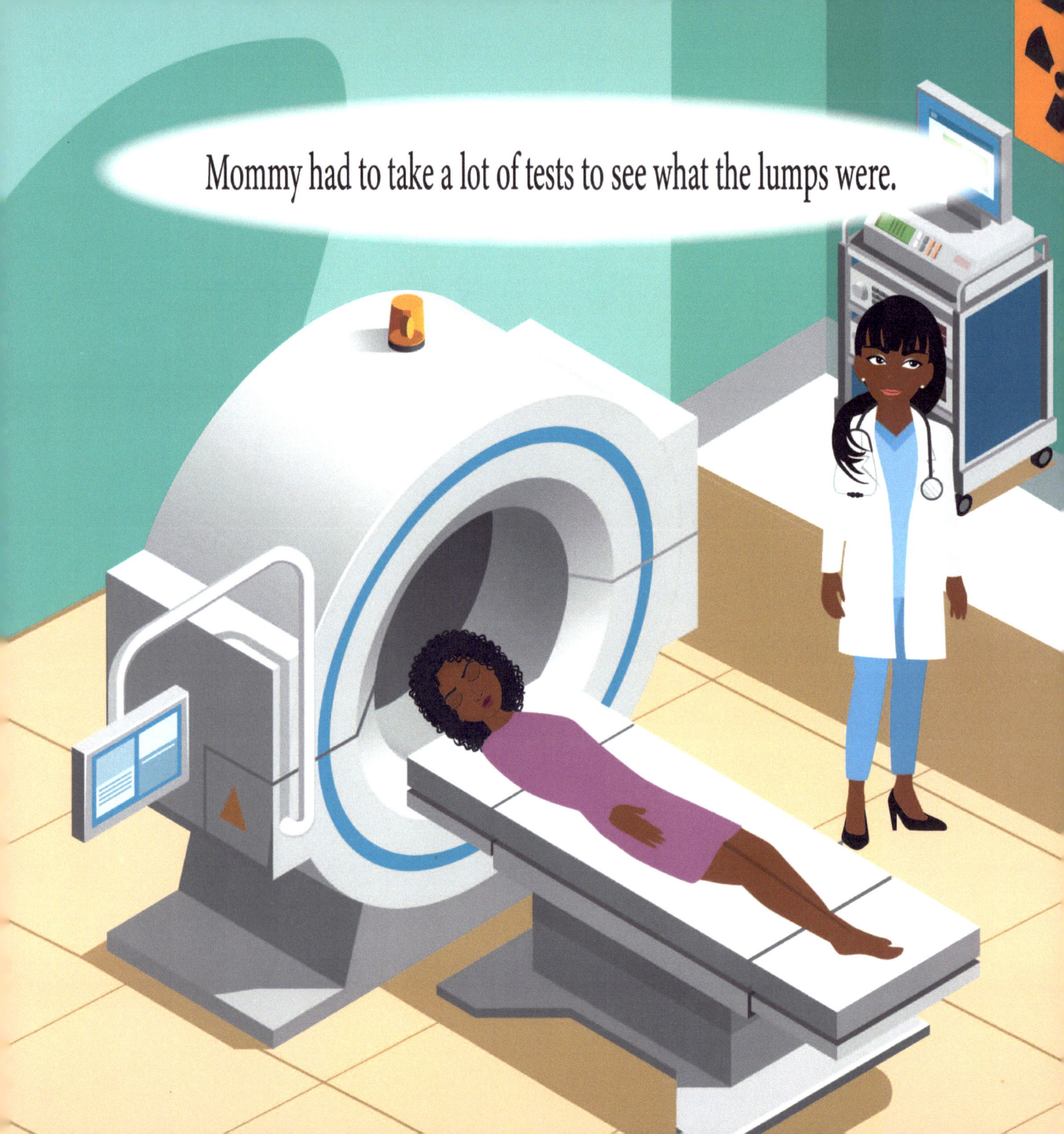

Nana looked sad, but I didn't know what treatment was and why it made her sad to hear that Mommy had to do it.

Mommy told us that she had breast cancer but not to worry. She would be okay!

Our Auntie Toy went with Mommy to all her appointments to see the oncologist, a doctor that takes care of cancer patients. Auntie took notes of what the doctor told Mommy. She emailed the notes to all the family and close friends so Mommy wouldn't have to tell everyone again and again.

Mommy had to have a surgery called a lumpectomy to take the lumps out. She said the lumps don't belong there.

After surgery, we gave Mommy balloons, hugs, flowers, and gifts. Then she went to her godmother's house to rest and be taken care of.

Mommy started chemotherapy a few weeks after her surgery. She said it made her feel icky, so Daddy drove her there and home. That way, she could relax.

After Mommy's 2nd round of chemo, her hair started to shed a lot. One night she was brushing it, and she got two bald spots in the front. She secretly said to herself it was time for a haircut!

I saw Mommy trying on a wig and ran down the street screaming and crying. I didn't know she was bald, so I was afraid. Mommy hugged me and let me know it was going to be okay.

Our Aunties gave Mommy a hat and scarf party the next day. She was so excited!

Family and friends came together to model the hats and scarves they brought and shared their favorite moments with her.

Grammie came over a lot to play with us, cook for us, and take care of her. One day Mommy was so weak that Grammie had to take her to the doctor.

Nurse Julie was upset with Mommy for not going to the doctor sooner. She said, "I don't want you tough. I want you well!"

We were all so happy. We called Papa, Mema, Mommy's best friend Brandi, and a few others to let them know what the doctor said.

Mommy still had to have more surgeries to be all the way better. She told us that she had to get new boobies, and we had to be gentle with her.

We were sad because we didn't want her to hurt anymore. But she said crying was not allowed because she would be okay! So, instead of crying and being sad, we smiled with Mommy and prayed for her.

And NOW………….. Our Mommy HAD Cancer, but she doesn't anymore!

The doctor told Mommy she couldn't have any more babies... But three years later, she gave birth to a baby brother for us.

www.ingramcontent.com/pod-product-compliance
Lightning Source LLC
Chambersburg PA
CBHW041704160426
43209CB00017B/1742